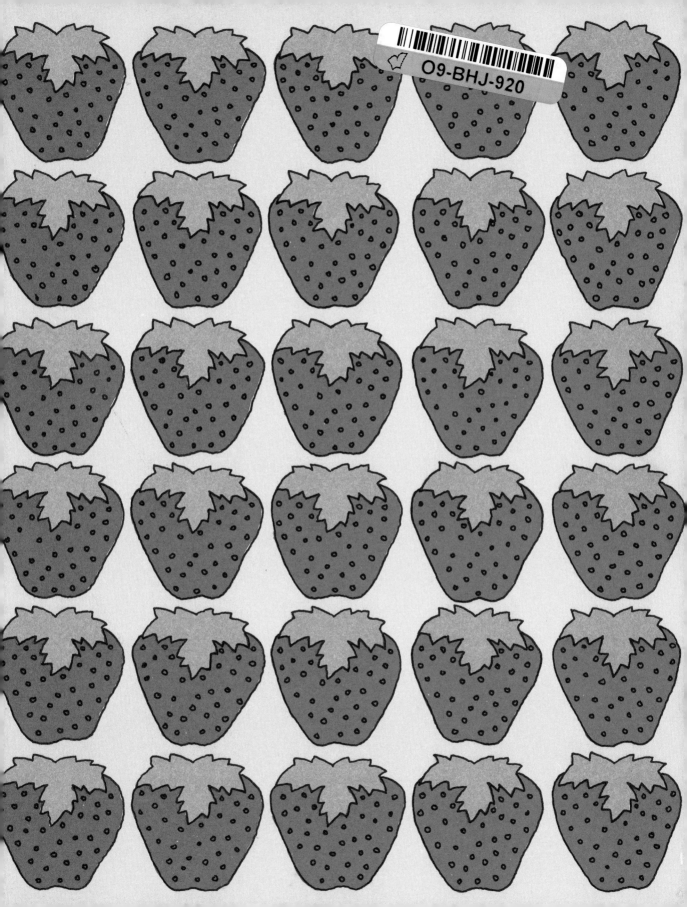

this
strawberry library
of first learning
book
belongs to

WILSON'S WEE WONDERS
DAY CARE SERVICE
263 Longstreet Drive
Gettysburg, Pennsylvania 17325
717 334-7493

*this book
is for
Pauline,
the grandmother*

Weekly Reader Books Edition

an animal alphabet

by Richard Hefter

a strawberry book®

A DIGNIFIED DONKEY
IS DRIVING A DUMP TRUCK.

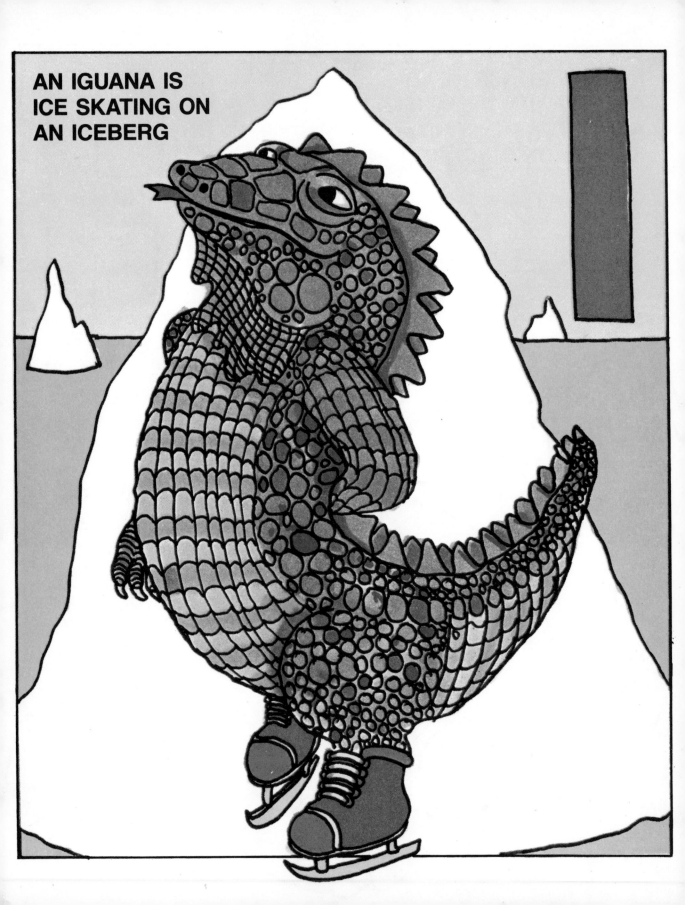

A UNICORN UNICYCLIST UNDER AN UMBRELLA

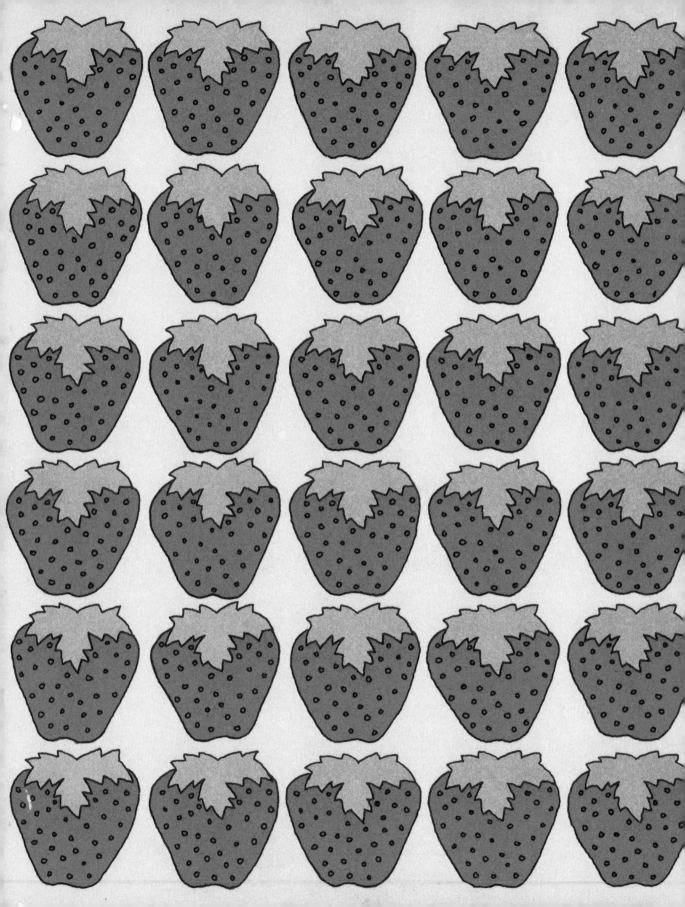